A Day Without Sun

A Day Without Sun

A Day Without Sun is a Collection of poetry, prose, by
Michael Tavon.

All pieces are original and were written by the
author.

The illustration created by Woe89s may not be reused
without the artist's consent.

Copyright 2018

Michael Tavon

Dedication

This is dedicated to the special people
who were there for me during my darkest
hour. Even if they didn't know. I also
deeply appreciate my supporters. The kind
words of appreciation you all send to me
every day keeps me motivated to keep
pushing. This is the end of my sadness and
I thank you immensely.

A Day Without Sun

TOC

Lip Service
The Void I
Part Time Lover
Why don't you love me?
I F*cked Up
Eviction Notice
Lifting
Friends with Benefits
Guilty Pleasure
Here it Goes
Sex
Lies
The Devil
In Case I Die
Writers Block
W.Y.L.S.Y.C.F.O.E.A.I
Y.N.B.Y.C.F.S.I
M.L.T.D.F.R
Real Life Hero
The Black Plight
Why Can't I Sleep

Michael Tavon

Insomnia x3
In The End Death Wins
Sadness
The Desert
Grief
Seek Help
Welders
Crazy
The Vultures
Time Machines
Alone With My Shadow
The Real
In Magic
To Be Human is to Know
Water
Consent
Dream
I Love Being Alone
Racism
Reprogram
Earth
Gold Plated
Assured
Be Selfish

A Day Without Sun

To Those Who Need It
Come Close
Old Me, New Me
Real Anxiety
Winter Season
I Don't Mind Dying
Love On The Dancefloor
Damn
Sleeping keeps me Alive
Life of Sheep
Crazy Drunk Sad
Poison is Pleasure
Just do it
The Media
Track 9
Happy Tears
Thanks for Teaching Me
You Deserve to Be Free
Earthquake
That's All I Need
Lithium II
LeadHer
My Shadow
Thinking to Myself

Michael Tavon

Til The Fucking Wheels
Everyday Is Halloween
Comeback...again
Maybe, Hopefully
The Pressure
A Lovely Place
The Ghost
We Rested Together
I Couldn't Sleep
Next To You
Dear Beautiful
The Irony
Maybe, What If
Late Night Action
A Great Woman
Let's Grow Together
Let Me Inside
Peace
Nothing Can Replace
Flames
Provider
Bloom
Wonder Woman
Fearless

A Day Without Sun

Skydiver
Dear You
Eviction Notice II
Drunk Love
It's Life

Michael Tavon

A Section for Late Night Yearning

Lip Service

Fill my ears
with sweet nothings
even if they're strawberry lies

Tell me I'm special
even if I mean nothing to you

tell me I'm everything
tell me I'm the world to you
when I'm just a past time.

I need to feel wanted
so look me in the eye
with the warmest smile
and say,

"you'll be fine."

Please be sincere when you do

The Void I

Loneliness has turned
into a hollow hole

    I fill with sorrow and drugs
    crushed by your numbing love.

I get high to escape
I get high to erase
but when I come down
I fall right back into the same place

    That hollow hole
    you gashed through my aorta.

I'm feeling colder without your touch
because you were my drug
but I'm strong enough to forgive
because I miss your love.

A Day Without Sun

Although your deceit
is what lured me in
i'd fall for it all over again
just caress you skin

Despite the fact
you've replaced my bed with his
i'll be around
to let you know
my undying infatuation
would never die.

I refuse to subside like a low tide
my eyes spread as wide as fire
when I catch a glimpse of your smile

I miss the way you say my name
I miss the way you rub my chin
that's why I'm willing
to bury my shame

4

just to have you again.

I'll apologize for your mistakes
i will suppress my disdain
to be in the comfort of your warm
embrace.
your grace, you left without a trace
all i have left are the fading memories
you left astray.

    But will I let them die?
    hell no not I
    i would rather dwell in our past
    than to ponder our present

Since you vanished
i'm suffering with the feeling of
severance
but my heart is still here
waiting for that void to be filled.

Part Time Lover

you're like the moon
only present when dark
providing comfort
as I rest my dreamin' eyes
and weary body.

    the moment I wake
    you vanish like a swift wind
    as the sun smiles
    through the blinds
    i still find myself reaching
    for you.

in my half-empty bed
i anticipate your arrival.
i spend my day fantasizing
of your scent
your touch

i count down the hours
minutes and seconds
until you arrive
undressed in my presence

you give me all of you
but only half the time
i'll settle for a part time love
it's better than nothing
at all

Why don't you love me?

you come as you please
and leave nothing
but the traces of your
body on my bed

i shut my eyes
to imagine
the last kiss we shared
before you drifted away.

I F*cked Up

I hope he treats you
the way i never did
while i had your heart,
you deserve it.
I got too comfortable
taking your affection for granted.

When your lips needed to speak
i muted your thoughts

when tears rained
i didn't provide sunshine
after the storm.
my pain became yours
then I pushed you away
as crippling it is to say
you deserve better
you got it
and I'm genuinely happy for you
so, farewell
I'll be better next lifetime

Eviction Notice

you've been living rent free
in my mental space
and it's time for you
to move you away.
you're dead weight
in a place that's at capacity
sorry, old friend
you need to go elsewhere
give me the key
and I'll be wishing you well.
goodbye.

Lifting

A huge weight was lifted off my chest
the moment I forgave the ones who tried
to break me

Friends with Benefits

we enjoy being lonely together

we're obsessed with the feeling

of tenderness

but afraid of falling

for someone new

so we enjoy these moments

knowing that's all they'll ever be.

we think this is the easy route

but soon we'll see how heart wrenching

this love affair will end.

Guilty Pleasure

We're not good for each other
but at night we're good to each other

    Natural sex
    wet kisses
    nude cuddles
    & deep pillow talk

    This affair, we share
    is a time bomb
    rapidly ticking
    til it implodes

We know, but the future doesn't matter
when present pleasure
gives us a high no drug can replace

A Day Without Sun

The thrill, the chase
we fuck like we're in love

    But become distant the moment
    I walk out the door
    we should call it quits

But the flower between
your thighs, reminds me of spring
Warm, blissful, and moist
I'm willing to risk it all
to hear the moan
of your voice

    My guilty pleasure
    I can't stay away

Here it Goes

So many women vie for my attention

but I can't afford to pay

my span is in dire straits

I want her and her too

she's beautiful but she's gorgeous too

who do I choose?

why should I have to?

I'm young and free

why should I be tied down to one

til I'm grey.

A Day Without Sun

What I'm trying to convey
is my pure affection for women
their energy is my addiction
therefor one, won't do the trick
for now at least.

I'll settle down, eventually
but there's so much
i must discover about myself
as well as the women around me

Women are life and I must explore
what they all have to offer
before settling down

Sex

Ever been so comfortable with a partner
that you spark a good convo
while boning and groaning?
Something about it stimulates me.
It's a rush I never thought to chase.
As I'm stroking and she's moaning,
suddenly we begin to
discuss, future goals, past fears and
brunch. As my mind goes into overdrive,
my lust does too.
Hearing her voice, while stroking
inside her warmth
I experience a climax, sexually and
Mentally.

<u>Lies</u>

You hurt me more
With the things you don't say
Versus the things you do.
As you hold back
The truth
I remain blissfully dumb
By the lies your body tells.

Michael Tavon

A Section for My Truest Thoughts

The Devil

The devil loves when you self-loath
It's pleasure to his dark soul,

When he sees your
Hope slowly burning away
Like the fire pit, in which he lays
He laughs at your pain

You scream and run
But find only
His red stare
Lurking amid the shadows

He feeds off fear
With teeth, wet of blood.
He doesn't chase
He waits for you give up.

20

So please keep running
Keep throwing punches
This will be the difference
Between eternal darkness
and lucid sunlight
Fight for your life.

In Case I Die

In Case I die soon
Please tell me you love me, too

I need to know the truth
before my spirit fades into the sunset

Don't hold it in today
Tomorrow may not exist

Yesterday is dead
And all we have is this moment.

Don't waste it
Biting your tongue,
with a stiff upper lip.

Tell me what I need to hear before
I disappear, say you love me, too

Writers Block

I try to find reasons why
to remain alive
but my paper remains white

No ink spill
or trace of thought

I've drawn a blank
no mistakes to erase

My thoughts have been trapped inside
this pen i shake to get them out

But I'm only
left with wasted time and doubt.

When you lose someone you care for
Or even an idol

Denial becomes your best friend
When the truth turns into
your greatest enemy,
As your ears combat
The words they
Refuse to hear
The first things you say are
"Stop playing" or "No Fucking Way"

Once the news is confirmed
The truth starts to sink in
Like a broken boat lost at sea
Suddenly you find yourself drowning
In your own tears,
Reaching for comfort,
Each breath becomes more important

Michael Tavon

As you swim to shore

Then you attempt
to negotiate with God
Hoping you can convince him
To give that person a contract
extension,
God denies your pleas and cries

Because you're afraid to sleep alone,

Anger finds a new home
Inside of you
Once your mind spirals
Into thoughts of regret
Wishing you could've done more
But it's not your fault,
Fate is never late to its appointments

When then truth comes back,
You listen to its words,

A Day Without Sun

despite the hurt
You laugh about the good times
And smile the moment you realize

They'll be fine
In the next lifetime
And you two will meet again

You're not black, you can't fucking say it

Simple as that
I don't care if you're only
black friend gives you a pass
he's as ignorant as you
I don't care if
say it with an a, not er,
It doesn't negate the ptsd
the word has caused
Many still wear the scars,
Around their wrists like a bracelet,
I don't give a shit
If you're reciting a joke or lyric
You should skip it
You have no place to argue why
Or state your plea
Your view on this invalid to me

27

A Day Without Sun

I don't want to hear your perspective,
Until that word is used
As a weapon
To pierce through your soul
Leaving you hallow, weak,
and feeling less than a human
You don't get to use the word
At your convenience,
So, save the first amendment speech,
Until you know
How exhausting it is to be black,
Having to wear a mask
To make the world
around you more comfortable,
Until you know what it's
like to have
Skin that attracts cops
For target and batting practice
You don't get to say the word,
In any way
Or any context

Michael Tavon

Moments like this one don't feel real

When the oxygen in your lungs
suddenly decides it no longer
wants to stay,
You're left reaching for it to comeback
As it slips from your fingertips

The hands on the clock go on strike
and time stands still
Nothing feels real
As you beg the hours
To console you
But they're just as sad as you are

Your heart beats
a rhythm so heavy
You stumble as you walk
Because the weight is too hard to carry

A Day Without Sun

Your mind goes haywire
trying to process the news
You break a fuse,
yours tears learn how to away too
Your vision becomes distorted

Behind the mist
In disbelief ,
you rub them like your performing
a magic trick
That will make everything reappear

Sadly, You can see it, feel it
hear it, and even smell it
No matter what
your senses can never make sense
Of how real death is

Real Life Hero

This cruel world will try to make you
feel weak for caring, but it takes a
great deal of strength to love in a
hopeless place. Love is a superpower.

The Black Plight

Black families,
laugh at therapy,
while drowning our traumas
With drugs and booze,
We numb ourselves
To the pain
We are too ashamed
To express

Michael Tavon

Why I Can't Sleep

There's a ghost who loves to visit
every night around this time
its name is 'the past'
it haunts and floods my mind with doubt
Regret and haunting thoughts of self-
loathing

When it's around
time freezes, I lose sleep
When I close my eyes
a whisper tickles my ear
Its daunting voice
Sends chills down my spine

The past comes and goes
as it pleases
I try to move forward
but it reels me back in

33

Insomnia x 3

I can't sleep with these

tears in my eyes

voices telling me to end it all tonight

maybe they're right

i mean little to the people i love

an afterthought i've become

balancing hope on a tightrope

while holding steak knives

looking down, from up high

at my demise

Michael Tavon

People don't know the

angst that lies inside

so i pretend

to be numb to the pain

when i'm more sensitive

than a drop of rain

i splatter when i fall

now these thoughts

are stronger when sober

and i have no one to call

i'm all alone

a feeling i should be used to

In the end death always wins

You could put up a good fight
and swing and miss a thousand times
for ten rounds,
Once you tire out
Death will knock you down
On the first try

You may be as fast as a cheetah
and try to outrun death
But as soon as you run outta breath
He'll catch you,

And grab the oxygen from your lungs

As humans, we learn early
We are not stronger, faster, nor
smarter
Than death in the end
Death always wins

Michael Tavon

Sadness

It's like waking up
without the slivers of light
sneaking through the blinds
it's like sitting in a tub of ice
smiling as your body turns blue.
It's like falling asleep comfortably
numb after a day of emotional abuse.
it's like falling in love
to only find out
you're being used.

A Day Without Sun

Happiness is like rainfall
in the desert
and it rarely pours
but I pray every night
for a shower
to resurrect the flowers
that have turned to ashes and stone

and that's hope
when your surface has become
dry and filled with dirt
you still envision
the green plants
pink flowers
towering trees
and animals prancing
on the terrain.

–   *The Desert*

I've learned how to turn
Grief into a smile
Because I didn't want
You to suffer too.

—   **Grief**

Seek Help

All alone
In a room full of lies.
Sweat covered hands
And eyes filled with cries

The walls are closing
running out of breath
You've convinced yourself
You don't need help
A lie you will protect til the death.

Your friends
Your family
Miss your laugh
The old you has left
And is long gone.

Michael Tavon

"Please come home"
Your heart cries
Instead, you please
The voices in your mind

Before you pull that trigger
Swallow that pill
Submerge under water.
Gash your wrist

Please think about the love you
Will be leaving behind.
Don't do it!
Seek help

Welders

We find ourselves mending
The broken parts of our past
With strength and heat,
Life turns us all into to welders

Michael Tavon

Crazy

I've lost it, I must accept it
Embrace the fact
I'm not at peace with my life
Numbing myself to the truth
Hurts more than living in this fantasy
world

I've created for myself,
There's nothing wrong with being crazy
There's nothing weak
about having mental breakdowns

But living with my head in the clouds
is more detrimental than
Healing myself with the truth
One day I'll be happy
But today isn't today
And for once, I'm okay with that.

43

The Vultures

They love to vulture our culture
As long they're not getting
profiled by cops
Followed by store clerks
Or stereotyped by servers

They love to gentrify our fashion
Because They don't know
what it's like to be viewed as a crime
even when wearing a suit or dress

They love tans
and wearing makeup
In darker shades
Because they'll never experience
The way some may
clutch their purse
When they cross paths
with someone like me

They don't know
What it's like to be viewed

as a threat
and a subhuman

It's easy to mimic the beauty of our
blackness
When you don't have to suffer the
consequences that come with it

Time Machine

Time flies when you
Spend your days
Yearning for the past

Alone With My Shadow

Self-doubt is my shadow
Trailing every step as I progress
Through darkness
When I moved forward from the past
I look back to see him
Looming over my shoulder
To remind me I'm not alone,
He mocks my every attempt
To evade,
I tell myself I'm doing great
I say in due time
I'll see the light,
I won't go out without a fight
I throw punches with all my might
Hoping one will strike him down
He scurries
and disappears for a while,
Long enough to convince
My mind I'm finally free,
The joy is short lived

A Day Without Sun

When I see his image
Dark,
wide,
silent
But loud
Staring from behind
I sulk
At the thought
Of some day
Sharing the same coffin as him

Michael Tavon

A Section for How I Feel

The Real

Take me as I am.
I am not ashamed to express any of my
emotions.

How I feel, will always be real.

In Magic

What if I told you
Your smile will be restored
Your heart will mend
After breaking down —

What if I said
The grass will grow greener
after the storm

What if I told you
Pain is a moment that fades
Like each minute of the day
Would you believe me if told
you these things?

I hope so,
'Cause
Change is like magic
You won't see it
if you don't believe
In it

To be human is to know

You must fight to survive
Constantly at war against
People who look like you,
People who don't like you,
And even your own mind

You constantly
have to exhaust your energy
Combating and scratching against
The opposition
To protect everything you love
And stand for

Living our truth is a battle
Most of us die fighting
Half of humankind has lost its
Empathy and became an army

Water

You're resourceful
And refreshing
Like a woman's love
  Just like women you're undervalued
    And abused
Without you, life would cease to exist
Another thing, you and women have in
Common, too.

Consent

In 2017, we still must teach grown men
what consent means. It's a sad case.
Men seem only understand the rules of
consent when applied to the women in
their lives. Yet they'll sexually
assault a stranger.
Her clothes aren't screaming
'fuck me'
Her walk isn't an excuse to rape her.
Her body isn't an invitation to grope
her. No, she did not ask for it. You're
not entitled to sex
After a few dates. Or because you're a
nice guy. Respect her as a human. It's
a scary world. Women deserve the luxury
of being able to roam without worrying
about getting abducted and raped, too.

Dream

When you find yourself
Losing sleep over
Fear
Heartbreak
Death
Money problems
And Time
Remember how
Beautiful your world is while dreaming

I Love Being Alone

Walking down an empty road alone.
Phone on 'Don't not Disturbed'
Moonlight gleams through the winter
trees. Brisk wind breathing on the
leaves. I'm at peace. Sauntering, as
the stars guide my way.
Basking in the ambiance
While I play Sade.
Stray cats purring, crickets chirping
Bushes ruffling, possums shuffling.
life is sweet.
The most precious
moments are often free, but priceless.
The greatest advice

"Enjoy what you have today, because
tomorrow doesn't come twice."

Michael Tavon

Racism

Racism is a disease
often hereditary
fatal and infectious
it spreads swifter
than a bad rumor
then leaves a dark hole
like a tumor

what was once blatant
is now dormant, to the naked eye
those with this illness
may smile like everything's fine
but burning inside
with a flaming hatred
if you're not of their kind

A Day Without Sun

to this day
there's no rhyme or reason
how this came disease about
and the only cure is death.

I remain hopeful
that science will find a cure
because it's unfair
to feel the effects of an illness
I've never had before

Reprogram

A mental breakdown is a sign
telling you it's time to reprogram

your brain needs to be refined
give it a new diet.
consume less toxic television.
misinformed news and social media.
take control of your life again
you're the master of your mind
somewhere along the road you've
forgotten that.

Read more, meditate.
learn something new
find a new hobby
anything you need to do
to free you from today's
toxic reality

No one cares about Earth
Anymore

A Day Without Sun

our green grass
is brown with thin blades
the sky is smoggy and grey
the trees are weak and losing shade

our oceans, once blue
have been polluted into a muggy hue
animals are losing food
most endangered too

The air is toxic
No wonder why we're all sick

Slowly dying. Father Time-- torpid
Mother Nature- ferocious
They're tired of our shit.

-Earth

Gold Plated
I know the difference

between what's real
and a gold-plated friendship.

They both feel like 24 karat
at first but the more
you wear it.
you'll notice the luster fading
day by day

Until it's golden coat is gone
exposing the pyrite
you fell backwards for.

A Day Without Sun

Realizing I was empty
Because I never found myself
Was the best epiphany I ever had
Now being alone is more blissful
Than ever.

I no longer yearn for love from
Another heart as heavy as years before
Because I've finally learned
How to Love myself.

–   *Assured*

There's nothing wrong
with being selfish
with your time

your heart
your money
your mind

   people become leeches
   who suck you dry
   when you're too kind

But when you need
anything in return
they turn blind
to your smile
and deaf to your voice.
leaving you dead
and emotionless

-          Be Selfish

To Those Who Need It

A Day Without Sun

Your vibrant spirit
Does not need to fade too soon
You have a story of pain
Millions of women deserve to hear
Don't take that away from them
Your heart is humble
Your ears are always open
When you speak
I often close my eyes
So I can listen clearly
Your words are powerful,
The way you're willing
To give without a second
thought is rare.
please don't leave too soon
the world needs more of you

Your pain, your rage
the voices in your head
you must continue to battle

don't let them win.
people need you
you're special to me, too.

Where are you, my love
I'm in need of your love
while I'm here alone

i'm sure you're in the arms of
another.

I can't fathom someone
like you being alone, too.

    -- As selfish as this may be
       I anxiously wait

for your heart to get broken
or for you to break his
so that one mistake
can lead you to me.

   -          *Come Close*

   The old me
   is so far gone
   we rarely got along.
   When I tried to escape

66

he tied me down, but I got away.

My old toxic friend
My beautiful enemy
His spiteful stares and
Lighthearted envy.

I was fooled once before
I don't need him any more
Goodbye to the old me
My former friend
A relationship that needed to end

Old me, New Me

Real Anxiety

67

A Day Without Sun

Chill bumps on my skin

Covered by a thin

Layer of sweat

My heart

Attempts to escape

The confines of my chest

My knees lock

My throat dries too

These thoughts, these fears

Are latching on like parasites

Feasting on my sanity.

I feel drained

Michael Tavon

but will I succumb?
Giving up is the easy route
anyone can quit
the brave move forward

Anxiety is the bridge
one must cross to feel bliss
on the other side
this bridge is often vacant
because most refuse
to cross their fears.
Are you one of those people, too?

A Day Without Sun

Winter season

Frigid air
Full moon
Dark sky
It's silent, too

Reminds me of
My cold dark room.
A room without you

Michael Tavon

Even as it slowly kills me
The temporary bliss it gives
Keeps me running back
Love is my favorite drug

—   I Don't Mind Dying

A Day Without Sun

On this stage called life
too many men have
stepped on her
tried to change her pace
or moved off-beat.

So she dances alone
waiting for the perfect mate
who's infatuated with her rhythm

the partner who
wants nothing more
than to dance with her
without moving too fast.

–   *Love on the Dancefloor*

Damn

Michael Tavon

Life's most sacred joys
Have turned into a fucking circus
To amuse the blind.

      People fall into relationships
      To prove they can be less alone.
      Couples aspire to be
      social media goals

Popular artists no longer
create to breathe
They create for aesthetic
and fast money.

It's killing me to witness
Everything turn into
Uninspired garbage
      Everyone wants to be famous
      But few have passion.

dreaming is my escape
It keeps me sane

when my eyes close
reality no longer burns
and hell feels like home.

in my dreams
I become limitless
fearless and close to perfect

if I dream enough
my visions will manifest
into my reality.

•Sleeping keeps me alive

Life of Sheep

Sheep are a simple breed
they move at command
their lives – monotonous
with little flare

They follow the pack
and consume what's given
they live to work
and nothing more

Adventure – nonexistent

Sadly, most humans
have become sheep, too.
they're unaware
or don't care enough
to break the cycle
and that's worse.

A Day Without Sun

Alcohol and drugs
Are here to make
You feel less alone
Like the old flame
You run to when there's nowhere to go
You can always count on
Gin
Brown
Whiskey
Tequila

Just like the person who tore you apart
It's a toxic bond
you're afraid to let go of
You'd hate to face your problems
Sober and alone

Crazy. Drunk. Sad

Poison is Pleasure

Poison is pleasure in disguise
It comes in many forms
And easy to over-indulge.

You consume with no regard
Using it to cope
With your angst

It makes you smile
It makes you free
It makes you forget
But it's all temporary

Once that poison
settles in your stomach
It becomes a part of you
You become part of this substance
Which makes it harder to let go

A Day Without Sun

By the time the pleasure fades
You've come to find
Your pain piercing your heart again.

Your toxic habit
Doesn't help you cope
It only holds you back from healing.

Just Do It

Sometimes
Saying 'fuck it'
Will give you the courage
To do exactly
What your heart
Is begging you to do.

The media's mission is to make us
stupid. Fake news gets shared more than
positive news. They want us to binge
watch TV until our brains rot.
Commercials for alcohol are broadcasted
every forty seconds. They rarely
promote books or healthy living.
Mainstream radio plays the same fucking
songs. People know more about celebs
than they know themselves.
Fast food ads are plastered everywhere.
(Most) Popular artists no longer create
for themselves; they follow trends for
money. All of this is met with little
resistance because consumers follow
like sheep. America wants us to live
dumb and die young.

—   The Media

Michael Tavon

A Section for Peace

(Track 9)

Tired of being lonely
Come over hold me
Never let go
As I fall in to dream
Like inception
You know what's next is
You and I , naked
Not literally, mentally
Tell me
Where ya secrets be
You can keep 'em safe with me,
in my heart
is where they're mean to be
Mentally, I'm sleep
Because I'm living in a dream
When you next to me.

Happy Tears

Tonight, I cried
but my tears were
as warm as raindrops
on a sunny day.

As I allowed my smile
to illuminate this cold dark room
i saw hope for the first time
in the dismal abyss.

I once accepted an old fate
the fate that said
there was no escape
and i would spend

A Day Without Sun

The rest of my days
bitter. poor. alone
then I saw a sliver a light
and cried.
tears of hope

Now I know to climb
even if it's an inch
per day
until my trembling hands
touch the wet soil
until I feel the sun beaming on my back
up is the only way to go
so, tonight I cried
because I finally have a reason to
smile.

Michael Tavon

As a fantasy
you were
a goddess in my dream world
when my eyes opened
you exposed me
to your scars, not fully healed
and wounds
that still
gave a sensation of pain

As the fantasy wanes
you become more beautiful
than what my imagination
could see.

You've become... human
my love, with a pulse.
my affection for you is no longer
an illusion or something
i cling to during my idle time

A Day Without Sun

I've fallen for a real-life warrior.
rest in peace to the dream
you used to be
now rise, a woman
who can mend a broken bridge

– *Thanks for teaching me the real you*

You Deserve to be Free

Holding grudges
Bares a mental strain
While the person who
Caused the pain
Feels nothing

They live in blissful ignorance
While your thoughts boil with vengeance

Do your mind some justice
By setting it free

Earthquake

I love so hard
The ground *shakes*
When my heart beats for you

Michael Tavon

Turn off Netflix
Disconnect the cable
Put down our phones
Let the music play softly

Let me soak you in
Without distractions.

I want to fall in love with you
In the still of darkness
In the melody of silence
Just your sleepy voice
Raspy laugh
And ebony eyes gazing at me.

That's all I need, nothing more

A Day Without Sun

My nerves shake
but I won't crack
Stormy thoughts may rain
but I mediate to clear my brain

Self Loathing taps
my window
i close the blinds

Self-doubt screams
in my ear
so i turn the music up

Nothing will stop me
i'm too much of a force to slow down
i'm in love with myself
and infatuated with
who I'm becoming

-Lithium II

<u>Leadher</u>

Lead her to a place she's never been

but don't drag her through

hell to *get* there

<u>My Shadow</u>

To the silhouette figure
 who follows
but never speaks
it's a reflection of me,
often larger than life
and appears
when there's a sliver of light

Posted on
the wall, so calm
stern, and self-assured
in ways it's
everything i'm not

Michael Tavon

It comes and goes
as often as the wind
but it's always on time
when I feel alone.

My shadow
my shadow
how you been here since birth
i've never heard a word
but your wisdom.
is well beyond
what my life suggests

Thinking to Myself

I wish i could be a woman for a day
so I can learn their pain
understand the strength it takes to
survive
under fire every 24 hours

What it's like to be a woman
in a world of chaos
in which they're reduced to silence

Only for a day I wish to be
a woman
because I doubt
i'd be strong enough
to endure the stress
much longer than that

Michael Tavon

I will *chase*
After your *love*
Until I heave from my empty
Lungs for fresh air
Giving up, never an option
I don't care
if my ankles swell
Or if I tear an ACL
I will crawl if I have to
To have you
Call me crazy
For being determined
That's fine
I left my sanity
Behind miles ago

– **Til the Fucking Wheels Fall Off**

Everyday is Halloween

Some people wear masks to cover the
insecurities that mock them when they
glance at their flawed reflection

Others shield their face behind masks
to hide their lying eyes from the
hopeful souls they gaze upon

Others wear masks to feel secure in
world that's eager to tear their heart
apart the moment they expose their
scars

Others may wear masks
To muster to courage
to save the world around them
People wear masks for many reasons
under the guise of fun and sin

Michael Tavon

To evade the truth
Like a crooked politician

Weather it be
Fear,
Insecurities,
Manipulation,
Or
Protection
We wear masks
To hide who we truly are,
it's ironic
We celebrate
A day of pretending
To be something
we wish we could be
'Cause we hide from
the truth year 'round

A Day Without Sun

The chase for your
Requited love
Intoxicates me more than
Any bottle ever could

The emotional
Firestorm you spark inside of me
Burns more than a dirty syringe
Piercing through my vein

I'm addicted to the pain you give
I can't feel my chest when
You speak to me

The way you come and go
My heart must be your favorite sport
Because you play me every season.

Michael Tavon

When it's all said and done
You casually leave
Without caring about the casualty you
left breathless.

– come back.... again

<u>Maybe, Hopefully</u>

Maybe I was wrong
Maybe I was too willing to give
you my all
without letting you in

Maybe I was too
head over heels
too soon.

Maybe it's my fault
for dreaming of our love
before seeking a reality, with you.

Maybe my strong will
turned you off.

Michael Tavon

Maybe I should have learned
to be your
friend
before fetishizing a romance

Maybe one day i'll learn
from these mistakes
maybe we'll see each other again

The Pressure

The pressure to love you
Was a weight I could not carry.
Which is why I folded
when you needed me.

One day,
You will find someone
Who won't feel any pressure to love
you.
Because it will be natural
To them.

Michael Tavon

Hell begins to feel warm
When you make it a home
Dwelling in a lake of fire
Turns into a refreshing swim
After a while.

A Lovely Place in Hell

The Ghost

Goodbye to
the ghost who taunted me
when I had nowhere to go

Goodbye to the ghost
the ghost who found me
as I dwelled in self-pity

The ghost who tortured my soul
when I yearned for a love
that wasn't for me

The ghost who once gazed
over my low shoulders
laughing as i sulked
in my own anxiety

Michael Tavon

Goodbye to the ghost
who was once my only friend
goodbye to the ghost
who lived inside my head

The ghost who whispered
bad advice at night

It's time to say goodbye
to the ghost
so I can move on
and fulfill
my purpose in life

A Day Without Sun

A Section for My Broken Heart

Michael Tavon

We Rested Together

She rested her mind on my chest
it was so heavy
my heart worked
overtime to stay composed

She fixed her tender lips
and said with her raspy
4am voice
"I feel as if you're greater than what
you show me."

    I was silenced
     she was right

This whole time
i was holding back
making it impossible
for her fall in love with me.

    She's brilliant
     and I love her for it.

A Day Without Sun

The average person
Falls in love with the idea
Of someone
But she's rare
And deserves to learn
the scars she doesn't see.

I kissed her forehead
Ran my fingers through her hair
Wished her goodnight.

She fell asleep
On my arm
Leaving me with one hell of a
Smile on my face.

- *I couldn't sleep*

Michael Tavon

With little effort
You put a hold on my heart
It beats patiently, for you.

Each moment
We share is intimate, to me
That's how deep
The water runs
In my well, for you.

Even in silence
I treasure every
Breath you take

A Day Without Sun

When you sleep

I stare at your bare face

Then dream of waking up

Next to you.

—   Next 2 You.

Dear Beautiful,

Wish you seen my face
when you wrote
"I'm blessed to have you"

    I rubbed my eyes
    to ensure it was no mirage
    sweet surprise
    deep down, deep down
    it will remain
    deep down,
    love

don't let it be a lie I read your soul
through each message
my heart thumps at those smiley faces
i hope the energy never fades
never fades...

Lessons and mistakes
heartbreaks and failures
have lead you to this place
here with me

So, I have no regrets
this bond would not
be possible.
nor would you be the
woman I adore, today
if that pain didn't exist.

If those mistakes
never took place
we'd still be lost
trying to find someone
who wasn't looking for us.

Michael Tavon

I praise your failures
i'm in love with your mistakes
obsessed with your pain.
i thank GOD
for it all
your detours, lead to my path.

The Irony....

A Day Without Sun

Maybe I should stop
dreaming of you and i

Maybe this dream
keeps me going
maybe the THOUGHT
of loving you is inspiring enough

Maybe there's 2%
of me who believes
you'll love be me back.
maybe I'm a fool
for wanting you
what if I don't mind
being a fool over you

What if I'm willing to risk
getting broken by you
what if I think
you're worth the risk

Michael Tavon

What if there's no risk at all
because you're the gem I've been
digging
For all along
Maybe
What if
What if
Maybe

All the if's in the world
all the maybes
I could think of
while I rest in this cold dark room
will mean nothing

– Maybe, What if

A Day Without Sun

Falling to sleep
Inside of you
There's no warmer place

–   **Late Night Action**

Michael Tavon

A Great Woman is Never Easy

She doesn't give in easy
I know she's worth the effort

I'll offer my heart
For as long as it bleeds.
It only beats to the rhythm
of her delicate strut.

The thought of having her
Is the glue mending
My broken hope
On this burning globe

My love is for her
Even if I never receive any
in return

A Day Without Sun

I aspire to love you
I aspire to grow with you
I aspire to be your husband
For eternity
Not even death would do us part

I aspire to get you higher
Than any drug
And reach nirvana without dying

I aspire to
Assist you with your fears
And help you forget how pain feels.

I aspire to nourish
My mind, body and spirit
To fill the well of your heart

– Let's Grow Together

Michael Tavon

Your body is here
but your mind is miles away
In my bed we lay
your thoughts wander
My distant lover.
come closer
I wanna get to know you

—Let me Inside

Peace

Be my peace in a state of war
Be the thread
Where my heart is torn.
Be the muse
When my thoughts are dull
Be the sensation when I feel numb

Show me your love
And I'll reciprocate it
With every breath in my lungs
Together we'll grow
Strong, so strong
A hurricane won't
Be able to tear us apart

I can't wait to get you near, my dear.

Michael Tavon

I have a lifetime of love give
Without fear.
In the meantime
Stay gold and continue to grow

Nothing Can Replace

A friend who cares
when you're hurt.
a friend who gives
with no incentive.

a friend who's strong enough
to lift you up when your knees
hit the asphalt.
a friend who supports
Your every endeavor unconditionally

A friend who doesn't wait
Til you're gone to say *I love you*
A friend everyone deserves
        A friend like you

Michael Tavon

Slow dancing with you
surrounded by flames
is the only way
i desire to leave this world
As we toe tap by embers
under a burning tree
we gaze into each other's
stare without a care
because a love like this
will survive in the afterlife.

– **Flames**

Provider

Alone with you
in the dark
only the sound of your voice
and the beat of my heart.
your head on my chest
more intimate than sex

"I love you" I say

As we kiss
i've dreamt of those lips
locking with mine
a thousand times
it was everything and more.

My guard is down, yours is too
i'll plant the seeds
watch the flowers bloom

nothing feels warmer
than lying next to you.

<u>Bloom</u>

Share your pain with me
      and I'll do the same
      We'll watch our wounds heal
    the way a broken rose
    blooms after it rains

Michael Tavon

Wonder Woman

In a world that has become
morbid
she continues plant
this tainted soil
with her seeds of passion
and waters them
with her tears of healing
then dawn light
with her smile of joy

in a world
fueled by hatred
she continues to spread love
over dry oceans
and dead grass
in an effort to revitalize
humanity's dying spirit
She's wonder woman, indeed.

Fearless

You're damaged
From the pain
life has put you through
        Despite it all
        You give a divine love
        Through a heart that aches
You're fearlessness
In its purest form.

Skydiver

A love unrequited
Feels like skydiving
Without a parachute
Hoping your partner catches you

Dear You,

You want to know why I keep my true
self contained in a glass bottle, for
you to see but can't touch.
It's because you hurt me once.
For years I watched you
Create memories with another man
Heard of you planning your future with
him. You loved him the way you were
supposed to love me. I was jealous.
I admit. I was jealous.
"That's supposed to be me" I would
say.

I tried to appear unbothered
I tried to seem over it
But I was broken.
You said we would always remain friends

Michael Tavon

But you never kept in touch
the more you fell for him
We faded day by day
No text messages. Calls. Invites. My
number was no longer saved. You and I
were just a ghost of yesterday.

If we were truly friends
Why'd you disappear?

Every woman i laid with or dated
Were replacements. These feelings I
tried to duplicate for other women who
were cheap imitations. You were always
on my mind.
These feelings, I thought were gone
Until you appeared at my front door.
I fell for you all over. After three
years of not being in touch. I'm
thankful you're in my life again.
Please excuse me if I seem hesitant. I
hope you understand.

A Day Without Sun

I forgive you for hurting me. I know
you didn't mean it. You wouldn't hurt
me on purpose. I didn't deserve you
then.
I don't deserve you now, but at least
I'm better than I was before. That
should count for something
What I'm saying to you is. I love you.

I don't know where we'll be five years
from now. Hopefully lying next to each
other. In our minimalistic home. You
smell so sweet. Nothing would bring
more joy than waking up to that face
every morning. And those lips are
everything I dreamt of

Our journeys
Will be taking different paths soon
But no matter how far
We go promise to never leave me, again.
And I promise to always be around
I'll wait for you

Michael Tavon

If I must.

Forever yours, Michael Tavon

Eviction Notice II

It's time for you leave
You've been living
In my mind far too long,
I stored
the memories we shared
In a carry on
So you can carry on
And hit the road,
It's difficult for me
to let you go
But allowing you to
stay on my mind
is killing me more
So please move faraway
From my mental space
Take care, stay safe

Drunk Love

My heart was
drunk off the thought
Of being in love with the wrong one

It's Life

In case you were wondering, I did not get her, but she's still my dear friend and I will treasure our relationship forever. Sometimes it's best to not get what you want. Sometimes there's a blessing in rejection.

If you're reading this I wish you well on your journey. If you ever need me, I'll be here. Love you.

Michael Tavon

End. . .

I feel so pure. So refreshed. I've
gotten everything off my chest. I'm
free now. Writing this collection
was so therapeutic. Time to move on
the next, Thank you all for ready,
and thank you even more for being
apart of my journey, Godspeed.

Michael Tavon

Other Works

From a Cold Dark Place
Love and Other Things
God is a Woman
Nirvana: Pieces of Self-Healing
Handle with Care

A Day Without Sun

Made in the USA
Middletown, DE
05 March 2021